T0209772

# Spirit Horse

### *and Other*
# Children's Writings

*NOT JUST A COLLECTION OF SHORT STORIES,*
*Children's Edition (for Adults and Children)*

## Anne Wilson Schaef, PhD

# SPIRIT HORSE AND OTHER CHILDREN'S WRITINGS
## NOT JUST A COLLECTION OF SHORT STORIES, CHILDREN'S EDITION (FOR ADULTS AND CHILDREN)

iUniverse books may be ordered through booksellers or by contacting:

iUniverse
1663 Liberty Drive
Bloomington, IN 47403
www.iuniverse.com
844-349-9409

ISBN: 978-1-6632-0214-7 (sc)
ISBN: 978-1-6632-0215-4 (e)

Library of Congress Control Number: 2021924543

Print information available on the last page.

iUniverse rev. date: 01/06/2022

# Contents

# Introduction

This book is not *about* children per se. I have always believed that adults need to read children's books because *they*, the adults, need to read them. We have all heard about "the child within". . . Well, I don't put much store in that, and I do believe that part of the problem with our society today is that most of us have had inadequate, if not non-existent, parenting and teaching as children. It's not anyone's fault. This aberration is just how our society has evolved.

It is because of the above, that I believe that children's stories and reading children's stories to our children are so important. Both parents and children need to learn the practical (moral) lessons of children's stories again and again.

Not only are children's stories fun, they often touch us at a deeper place that words alone find difficult to reach.

Don't be frightened if a tear starts to trickle down your cheek when you read some of these stories. Crying can be a very good and intimate thing to do together.

The above does not imply that children's stories cannot be read alone by adults. They can and should be. I promise you no harm will come to you if you do this.

You may be in danger of a chuckle, a laugh, a memory, or a flow of tears, and . . . that can only be good for all of us.

There is also a wee possibility you'll pick up some important clues about living well. What's the problem? Try it. You'll love it! And if you don't, that's a learning too. So what do we have here?

Here we have a book of children's poems and short stories for adults and children.

This book has something for us to return to again and again as we peel off layers toward healing, growing, learning, and insight.

Should we read it through? Perhaps.

Should we select certain titles at certain times? Perhaps.

Should we just read whatever pages the book falls open to? Perhaps. (You can't do that with an electronic book, and they too have their place.)

It's your book. Read it as you choose and as it fits for you at any given time.

I actually wrote all these entries for myself, and now I have decided to share them with you. Truthfully, almost all these writings were initiated by my muse, and I was the "hollow bone" that wrote them down.

# 1

# Rhyming Learnings

## Goo on My Shoe

Alas and alack!
Tell me—
What should I do?
I just put my foot down
In a big bunch of goo.
It's sticky, it's icky,
It's not very nice,
And the worst thing of all is
I've now done it twice.

To look where I'm stepping
Seems such a very small thing,
But I just get so busy—
To remember seems strange.

I'm playing, you see.
To look what I do
Just doesn't make sense,
But I get goo on my shoe.

Surely Mother will help me
To get rid of this goo stuff.
If she will just fix it,
I can then get in new stuff.

But what happens when Mom
Is just not around?
I may get stuck somewhere
And not get off the ground.

To watch where I step
Could be quite an advantage.
Then, when no one's around,
I can quite easily manage.

# Loving Lightning

How funny, how weird,
How strange and exciting.
I just saw a zigzag
Of red-colored lightning.

What a wonder it is
To look at a dark sky
And see it turn green
In front of my eye.

There's lightning that comes
With no cloud in sight
That covers the sky
In glowing white light.

There's lightning that screams
Through the air like a banshee
And lightning that whispers
And rolls—that we can see.

Some lightning comes down
In a jagged saw blade
All the way to the ground
And leaves footprints it's made.

Other lightning goes across
The sky in great billows.
When I look out my window,
I can see to the willows.

Lightning's a celebration.
Nature's wonder and delight.
We could never have wished for
A more glorious sight.

# Ants in Pants

I sat on an anthill,
And they made such a fuss
You'd think it was *their* place
And didn't belong to us.

They planned, and they gathered
To launch an attack,
Then swarmed all over me,
Going right up my back.

They bit, and they stung.
They pinched, and they fought.
They covered my body.
I was sure I was caught.

I went running to Grandma
With tears in my eyes:
"Those ants, Grandma, hurt me!"
She said, "What a surprise!

"Come over here, little one,
So you easily can see
Why the ants swarmed all over you.
It's how ants tend to be.

"You see, you sat down and destroyed
Their homes, village, and town.
When you sat on their anthill,
It all tumbled down.

"They only wanted to tell you
To take mind of them, to be
Watchful where you're sitting,
And notice them, you see.

"We all have to live together
In a very small space,
And if we don't notice others,
They'll put *us* in our place.

"To respect each little creature
And honor their homes
Means we can all live together
On this lovely earth dome.

"The ants were only trying
To remind you, you see,
That when everyone notices,
There's room for you, room for me.

"The Creator made all creatures
To teach us true balance.
No telling what would happen
If we notice the ants.

"Why, then maybe we'd notice
Other important things,
Like the trees, lakes, and rivers
Or the wild things that sing.

"And if we didn't notice them,
What a state we would be in.
Soon the world would be a mess,
Filled with ucky pollution.

"Then where would we grow
All these good things to eat?
Where would clear water flow
And the rain wash our feet?

"The ants *only* wanted to remind you
That they're important too.
We must all work together,
Respecting what *they* do.

"This earth is a great place,
A wonder to behold.
If we all live together,
Then we all can grow old.

"Knowing each has a place here,
We're all important, you see,
To the whole great big story
Of planet Earth—you and me.

"Now, the ants had a direct way
Of teaching you this lesson.
Let's sit here and cuddle,
And the stinging will lessen."

# Listen

Listen, my children,
and you will hear—
God knows what!
And
to be sure,
it will be
much more
than
if you
had not
listened.

# 2

# The Red-Footed Booby

"I'm so upset,"
The booby said
"These feet turned out
A fireman's red.
I simply know
Not what to do
They should have been
A lovely blue.
I will not have
Friends I can pick
Like every other booby chick
What does this mean
This glaring red?
I'd much prefer
Blue feet instead."

With bright red toes,
She went to play
Maybe a booby nose
Would make her okay.

"Just being a booby
Is surely bad enough,
But a red-footed booby
Is really hard stuff.
I just can't imagine
A worse thing to be
Than a small red-toed booby
Who looks just like me."

Her mother did say
"I'm so sorry, dear
It's your father's bad genes
They're all strange, I fear."
Her father rose up
With great indignation:
"Your family's the one
With the bad reputation!"
They fought, and they fought
Yet never could see
That this was no help
For a lonely booby.

With tears in her eyes
That did smart and did sting,
She wandered outside
But could scarce see a thing.
There sitting and rocking
Was an old Tutu booby
Saying, "I am your Grandma
You can sure trust me truly.

Come here, my dear child,
We are birds of a feather
We'll work this thing out
We'll do it together.
Don't sniffle. Don't sigh
We'll find a solution
Together, you and I
We'll create revolution.
Grandmas are special
If there's one thing they know,
It's how things used to be
When the world was more slow.

"Come crawl up right here
In my big booby lap
We'll tell stories, you and me,
Then we'll take a short nap."

Having a booby for a grandma
Seemed a very fine thing,
And one who could tell stories
Made her booby heart sing.

"A long time ago,
Before anyone remembers
The world was a cluster
Of red glowing embers.
The Creator looked down
At this wonderful sight

And said, 'My goodness, oh me,
That looks just about right!'
Then, after a while,
The embers glowed gray,
And the Creator discovered
They looked good that way
'I love that red color,
And gray looks good too.
I'll sit here and ponder
What next I should do.'

"As the Great Being thought
About where next to go,
The ember turned black
In a three-colored glow.
'How beautiful! How wonderful!
That's much better yet!
I wonder what's possible,
How many colors can I get?'
With a celestial paintbrush
Like a great big, huge broom,
The Creator began painting—
A swish here, there a zoom.

"'I'll make rainbows of people
And animals with spots.
Fishes with neon
And butterflies with dots.
There'll be beautiful flowers

With every known hue,
And they'll live together
Like me and like you.
There'll be great big green trees
Whose leaves will turn red
And others just like them
With yellow leaves instead.
Oh, isn't this fun?
I could never believe
The joy in just making
A bright-colored leaf!'

"The Creator continued
With fishes and bugs,
Bright-colored worms,
Black-and-yellow banana slugs.
'Whee! Isn't this something?
Each one a surprise.
I'll have to rest sometime,
Perhaps after sunrise.
I'll do creatures that fly,
Made with colorful feathers.
How creative am I?
This is fun altogether!'
So the Creator continued
Every day, every night,
To create beautiful creatures,
Each one a delight.
'Now, what can I do

To make special each one
So that everyone knows
To be different is fun?'

"You see, everyone's unique.
No one else is like you,
A most special creation
To live your life through.
Differences are magic
From the brush of the Creator,
Bringing joy and excitement,
And there'll be more changes later.
Creation keeps happening.
No day is the same
As the one just before it.
We all get to change.

"We boobies, for instance,
All used to be brown.
Then the Creator saw us
And gave out a big frown.
'I've neglected the boobies.
Goodness, what shall I do?
I'll give some striking red feet
And the others bright blue.
How beautiful! How wonderful!
Do you think they'd like spots
On those bright red and blue feet,
Or perhaps they'd like dots?

"'I'll just settle back
And wait till I know
If I need to make changes
And which way I should go.

"'I do like the boobies.
They're so beautiful and rare.
Brown-, blue-, and red-footed—
Quite glorious, I declare!

"'You see, each little booby
Is special to me.
Each little creature
Is beautiful to see.
I love all these differences.
What a great, wondrous lot!
So magnificent and changing
Is the world I have wrought.

"'I'll rest now, I think!'
And began a short doze,
Dreaming of red-footed boobies
With red booby toes.

"And that's how it is,"
Her grandma then said.
"Everyone is so perfect,
'Specially if your feet are red.
Each one is created
Super wonderful, super unique

We're all here to add color,
And even as we speak,
The wonder continues
As new beings arrive.
It's magnificently fabulous
To just be here, alive.
Each one is so special,
Whether fish, tree, or bird,
That to think we're not great
Is magnificently absurd!

"How lucky I am
To have you in my lap
Now, let's rock here together
And take our short nap."

*These feet aren't so bad,*
Thought the red-footed booby.
*The Creator made me special.*
*There's no other like me.*

How lucky she was
To just have red feet.
She suddenly realized
They were really quite neat.
No telling what the Creator had
In that magnificent head.
She could have had polka dots
Or neon instead.

To be as she was
Was quite a relief.
She'd make a note to herself
Not to cause so much grief.

Then she snuggled in close,
Feeling very content,
Knowing she would be happy
Wherever she went.


*A booby is a seabird found in Hawaii and the South Pacific. There are red-footed boobies, blue-footed boobies, and brown-footed boobies.

# 3

# Did Ya Ever Notice?

Did ya ever notice how grown-ups seem to sort of take over sometimes?

It was one of those great days with bright sunshine and only a few little, puffy clouds. I was tickled when my grandparents and father decided to pack a lunch and head for the beach. I slipped into my swim trunks, grabbed my swim ring and favorite "cane," and was ready to go. (It wasn't really a cane—it was a stick with a crook in it. I just liked to pretend it was a cane, and I used it for walking.)

When we got to the beach, I was so excited that I was jumping up and down. There was hardly anyone there, and we were almost going to have the whole beach to ourselves—freedom!

I was so eager to get to the water that I dropped my swim ring, and the wind caught it. It went flying down the beach, and I tore after it. I was really running fast, and I was sure I was gaining on it, but every time I almost caught up, it would take off again. I wasn't worried. I knew I would catch it. Actually, I could have caught it sooner, but I was trying to hook it with my cane, which was a little more difficult than just grabbing it.

Just when it hit the water and stopped, and I almost had it, my dad rushed in and got it. He thought he had stopped it. Can you imagine that? He thought he had saved the day.

I was willing to let that one pass. It seemed important to him that he thought he'd stopped it. I could handle that—no big deal.

Then, when we were walking back up the beach—we were both sort of winded from the run, and it was fun to be walking with my father—an old woman looked right at me and said, "Boy, you were really running fast." I was proud that she had noticed.

My dad answered, "Yes, I sure was. I've had my exercise for the week."

She hadn't been talking to him! I knew she had been talking to me. He'd answered as if she had been talking to him. Can you believe it? Did ya ever notice how grown-ups do that a lot? They answer for us, even when someone was obviously talking to us. Sometimes they don't seem to know what's our business and what's their business. They seem to think that because they're grown-ups, everything is their business. That got me to thinking—did ya ever notice this kind of thing happens a lot?

I started remembering times way back when I was really young a long time ago. Once, we were on our way to the beach when I was real little. I was sitting in my car seat and didn't talk much. There was a great big rainbow stretching across the whole sky. It was beautiful! I watched it a long time. Then one of the grown-ups finally saw it. They got all excited. They kept saying, "Look, Roddy! Look at the window." They were acting like they'd discovered it. Did ya ever notice how grown-ups think they discover everything?

We kids are really good at discovering things, you know!

Then there was the time when I was *really* young and was supposed to learn to eat. Now, the idea of eating, as I understood it, was to get the food from my dish to my mouth. Simple enough—no big deal. I wanted to check that out and see how many ways I could discover to get the job done.

I tried the finger-and-thumb method with tiny bits of food. That worked pretty well, but it was slow. If I hadn't been very hungry, it could have been fun, but a fellow could starve that way.

I tried the spoon method. The spoon could hold more food, but that silly thing had a mind of its own. Sometimes it just tipped over for no reason at all, and everything fell off. Then, other times, it was like it just did whatever it wanted, and it tried to poke that food into my eye or the side of my cheek. That didn't work too well, and it ... wasn't much fun either.

Then I tried the fist method. Now I was getting somewhere. I would just get a fistful of food and stuff it into my mouth. That worked great! I got more food faster, and my fist hit my mouth more often than the spoon did.

The fist method gave me a great idea. What if I just got rid of the in-between bother of a spoon or a fist and just plopped my head into the dish? That worked great, and there were all kinds of "extras" that stuck to my face that I could easily push in. I was quite pleased with myself.

But my parents had a fit. Here I had checked out all these different ways and found a way that really *worked*, and they didn't like it.

Did ya ever notice how grown-ups think there's only one way to do something? Their way.

Back to the beach. I like to build sand castles. One day I had been working a long time on a sand castle. The castle had a big hump in the middle, where I had filled my pail with sand, packed the sand down tight, and then turned the pail upside down and pulled it off. It made a great tower. It crumbled some, but that was okay. Most of all, I like digging in the sand, rolling in it, and feeling it on my hands and body. It tickles!

Anyway, I was working hard, and my dad came over and started changing my sand castle. Now, this is a tough one. I love it when my dad plays with me. Don't get me wrong—that's special! But I hate it when he doesn't *ask* if I want him to play with me and doesn't check to see if I want him to change my sand castle. He just does it.

Did ya ever notice how grown-ups just assume we want them to play with us, and they change something we are building without getting our permission?

We know what we're doing. We might like them to play *with* us, but we have ideas too, and maybe we need to be left alone with what we are doing or at least be respected and *asked* if we want them to play with us right then. It's a little thing, and it's important.

I think it's really important for grown-ups to see that kids can do kid things and adults can do grown-up things.

Sometimes I am having fun struggling with something, like trying to catch my swim ring, and I can handle it. I like knowing that I can rescue my own swim ring.

Most times, I can answer when someone speaks to me, and if I don't want to, I don't want someone else putting words in my mouth. Ugh, what a yucky idea.

I can discover, and I can experiment. I can explore, and I can notice. Kids are good at these things.

On the other hand, grown-ups are good at things too. Grown-ups are really good at loving us and cuddling us. They are great for keeping us from running into the street when we don't know any better, and they are great at giving us information and teaching us things—for example, they could show us different ways to eat and then let us try them out and discover new ways too.

I think things would really be great if kids could do what we do best and grown-ups did what they do best. It would make things a lot simpler and more fun for both. Don't you think so?

# 4

# Waddles

Waddles knew that it was a bright, sunny day, because he could see the sunlight through his eggshell. Also, the sun was so warm that if not for the way the sunshine lit up his egg, he might have thought his mother was still sitting on the bunch of eggs in her nest.

*My mother must have left the nest for a while and is letting the sun keep her eggs warm for her. She is probably feeding nearby,* thought Waddles.

Waddles decided that this was a good day indeed to be hatched, so he began pecking his way out of his shell. At first, it was harder than he'd thought it would be, and he realized that if he wanted to get out of his shell and surprise his mom when she came back, he would have to work hard at pecking.

Waddles was a strong little duck, and he knew he could break open his shell. He wanted to be all dry and fluffy when his mother returned. He pecked harder, and suddenly, the shell split open, and there in the bright sunlight stood a somewhat bedraggled-looking Waddles.

It took Waddles a few minutes to dry off in the warm sun. He stretched his little neck, shook each little leg, opened and closed his webbed feet, and extended and wiggled each tiny wing. *Enough!* My, it was good to be alive on such a fine day.

After Waddles made sure all his parts were in working order, he began to look around. Just as he had hoped, he was the first one to hatch. *My mother will be so proud of me*, he thought. Some of the other eggs were rocking a little, but none had even begun to hatch.

"I'll just peek over the edge of the nest," Waddles peeped quietly to himself. *Wow!* He drew his head back quickly and tumbled end over end back into the nest. Then, slowly, he inched up over the edge again.

Their home was right on the edge of a big lake. It was so huge that to a little duck like Waddles, it looked like something bigger than he could have imagined. Across the lake, in the distance, majestic mountains reached into the puffy clouds. It was spring, and the green grass was edged with forsythia and bougainvillea bushes with yellow, pink, orange, and deep red blossoms. *What a beautiful world my mother has chosen for her babies*, Waddles thought.

He looked around for his mother, but she was nowhere to be seen.

"I'll just slip over the side of the nest and look for her," Waddles chirped softly to himself, and over he tumbled.

Just then, a little black bug raced over Waddles's webbed foot, and Waddles felt a tickle. "He-he," he gurgled. "That feels funny!"

Then Waddles looked at the bug, and suddenly, he realized, *Hatching is hard work. I'm hungry!* He chased after the bug.

"That bug really can move, but so can I!" Waddles peeped confidently, feeling his newfound freedom and power.

Off he raced down the beach after this bug and that bug, tasting bits of grass and drinking the cool lake water. His world seemed safe and easy to handle when he was focusing on the bug. It was only when he looked up that he realized that he was out in a great big world ... alone.

"Mama! Mama!" he peeped, but there was no answer. He could not even see his nest or the other eggs. *I would give anything to snuggle against one of my brothers' or sisters' eggs right now*, he thought. *I don't even know which way to go.*

Suddenly, Waddles realized he was afraid. "Peep, peep, peep," he said very quietly. "PEEP, PEEP, PEEP!" he screamed. No one noticed.

Waddles sat down on the grass at the edge of the beach. He didn't know what to do.

"Where's my mother? She's supposed to be taking care of me." He began to pout. "I'm too little to be out here alone!" he wailed.

Then he realized that he was out there alone because *he* had wandered off. No one had done this to him.

"I'm too little to be learning this lesson about taking responsibility for what I do!" he cried.

Then he realized that he was learning this lesson whether he liked it or not.

"I'm too little to be sitting down and trying to figure out what I need to do next!" he bellowed. And then he realized that this was exactly what he was doing.

Just then, a mud hen ran by, obviously going somewhere in a great hurry.

*Maybe that's my mother*, Waddles thought, and he took off running after her. Even Waddles was surprised at how fast his legs could move.

Suddenly, the mud hen plunged into the cold waters of the big lake. Waddles knew he must follow her. Bravely, he waded into a big wave that looked ten feet high. He wasn't even sure he could swim.

The wave tossed him end over end, and he ended up back on the beach. Frantic, he saw the mud hen getting farther and farther away, and he knew he must be brave enough to try to swim again. He ran to the edge of the water, and when a big wave came, he dived into it … and … what do you know! He found himself on top of the water, riding the waves! If he had not been in such a state of panic about catching the mud hen, he could have realized how much fun he was having.

Waddles began to paddle furiously. His webbed feet were perfect for this. Much to his surprise, he shot ahead in the water, and he realized that if he paddled hard, he could almost skim on top of the water. "I'm almost flying," he peeped, swallowing some water. *Perhaps it's not a good idea to talk when I am swimming so fast in big waves*, he thought as his legs paddled rapidly.

Waddles was tiring, and beginning to think the mud hen seemed to have no interest in him at all. *Surely if that were my mother, she would let me catch up*, he thought sadly. He looked over his little wing to see a big, beautiful black swan gliding by.

*She's wonderful*, thought Waddles. *She is much more beautiful than that other bird. She's much more likely to be my mother.*

So Waddles turned around and began to follow the splendid black swan with the lovely red beak.

But the swan swam even faster than the mud hen, and she went even farther from the shore. Waddles was not sure if he could go farther out or if he could swim any faster, but he had a brave heart, and he would try. Off he went after the big, beautiful black swan.

The swan saw Waddles swimming frantically after her, and she thought to herself, *I wonder what he wants. Surely he does not think I am his mother. We swans would never produce a baby that little. He does swim well, though.* She glided around the dock to join her friends, who were feeding in the shallow water of the lake.

Suddenly, Waddles found himself surrounded by big black swans. They gathered around him. He felt terribly small as he looked up at their long necks and red beaks. Their heads looked as if they were attached to their bodies by long swivel cables. They could do amazing feats with them! They could stretch their necks way out in front of them. They could tuck their necks completely across their backs. It seemed to Waddles that they could look at him from every direction at once.

A large swan stood on one foot at the edge of the water with his long black neck resting back on his body and his head tucked under his wing. The swan was sleeping! *I could never do that*, thought Waddles.

But then he realized that he had a more immediate problem: he was out there in the water, surrounded by these big swans, and he had no idea what they wanted.

*I hope they don't eat little ducks*, he thought, suddenly realizing he was a duck and not a swan.

As he bobbed on the water, a long neck stretched his way, and a big yellow eye came close to his head.

"What do you want?" said the swan. "Why have you come out here with the swans?"

"I hatched early. I wanted to surprise my mother. I went looking for her, and then there were bugs, and then I was lost, and I tried to find her. I followed a bird I thought might be my mother, and then the swan went by, and she was so beautiful. I hoped she was my mother. I'm lost, and I'm lonely. I'm cold, and I don't know where my mother is." Waddles sobbed.

The kind old swan sighed. *Why aren't these little ones more careful?* he thought.

"Well," said the swan, "we both know you're not a swan, but I must say, you are a very strong, very brave, and very foolish little duck. We will escort you back to shore, and maybe you can find your mother."

Soon Waddles was back on the shore, tired, hungry, and afraid. It was starting to get dark. He also realized that when the sun went behind the mountains, it was not as warm as it was under his mother's warm, fluffy breast.

Waddles huddled down at the edge of the lake. He did not know what to do next.

"I should have waited for my mother to come back," he said. "I was just thinking of myself, and I was foolish."

Just then, he heard a quack and a chorus of peeps.

Down the beach came a mother duck and seven little ducklings. Four were bigger than the other three, but they all seemed to be getting along okay.

Waddles ran up to her excitedly. "Excuse me. Are you a duck?" he asked.

"I am," she said as her brood chattered wildly.

"Who is he? What does he want? Shall we peck at him?" they shouted.

"Wait a minute," said Mother Duck. "He's a duck just like you. Listen! What do you want, little fellow?" Mother Duck asked.

"I hatched early. I wanted to surprise my mother. I went looking for her, and there were bugs, and then I was lost, and I tried to find her. I followed a bird I thought was my mother, and then a swan went by. She was so beautiful. I hoped she was my mother. I'm lost, I'm lonely, I'm cold, and I don't know where my mother is!" Waddles sobbed.

"There, there," said Mother Duck. "You have had a big day—your first day of life.

You must be very tired," she said as she put a protective wing around him. He felt so safe—and then the noise began.

"Wait a minute. There are enough of us. You're not going to take him in, are you? We don't get enough attention as it is!" chorused her brood.

"Now, let's all of us wait a minute," said Mother Duck. "This duck is family. He needs a family. Where would all of you be if I hadn't been willing to take in two broods? What if this had happened to *you*? We have plenty to share."

The little ducks fell silent, realizing that they could have been in the same position as Waddles, and they would have liked to find a mother like theirs.

"You rest awhile, dear," said Mother Duck. "When you wake up, we will try to find your nest and your mother and brood. If we don't, you are part of our family."

Waddles sighed and snuggled into Mother Duck. It was nice to belong.

The next morning was a beautiful day, and the lake, the beach, and the mountains in the distance seemed familiar as Waddles stretched, yawned, and waddled down to the lake for a drink, keeping a close eye on Mother Duck.

"We'll walk down the lake and eat as we go," Mother Duck said. "I believe that a friend of mine, Mama Waddles, was just about to hatch some eggs. Maybe she is your mother. We'll see."

Waddles felt a familiar feeling when he heard the name Mama Waddles, but he didn't want to get too hopeful. And, he had a nice family here.

The duck family slowly worked their way down the beach. The older ducks explored farther away from Mother Duck, but she kept a sharp eye out and always called them back if they went too far.

Waddles, of course, stayed very close.

After a while, Waddles heard another duck quacking in the distance. "You wait here with the other little ducks, and I'll go check," said Mother Duck, hoping to spare Waddles any more heartbreak.

Soon she waved to the brood and told them all to come down to where she was.

As Waddles approached the nest, he could see that it was his nest, and he knew this must be his mama. "Mama! Mama!" he cried, rushing toward Mama Waddles.

Mama Waddles lifted her wing and gently pulled Waddles under it while she crooned softly, "Quack, quack, welcome home, my little one."

Mother Duck and Mama Waddles chatted while the babies played. Waddles was strong and a good swimmer. He could even swim as fast as the bigger ducks in the brood.

As it began to get dark, Mama Waddles invited Mother Duck and her babies to spend the night. Waddles didn't know where to sleep. *Should I sleep with my old brothers and sisters or with my new brothers and sisters?* he pondered. He felt so wealthy. He had two families!

Waddles was tired. He had been alive for only two days, and so much had happened.

That night, as they settled down, the two mothers and the baby ducks talked about many things. They all wanted to hear about Waddles's adventures. Waddles felt honored that the evening sharing focused upon him. He wanted to share what he had learned.

"I learned that I am brave and strong, I am a good swimmer, and that I can be foolish. I learned that there are kind beings, and there are also those who don't care about me at all. I learned that I am the one who wandered off and that I need to pay attention to what is safe for me. Most of all, I learned that adventures can be fun and scary, and it's better to do them with family. I am luckiest of all because I have two families—two mothers who love me and lots of brothers and sisters to play with."

Waddles closed his eyes, thinking, *I am a very lucky duck indeed.*

*This story is dedicated to a little duck frantically trying to find his mother on Lake Taupo in New Zealand. I hope his ending worked out as well.

# 5

# Old Brother Bear

Old Brother Bear sure wanted some of that honey the bees had made. He thought and thought about how good it would taste. The more he thought about it, the more he wanted it. The more he wanted it, the more desperate he became. Lots of animals wanted some of that sweet honey; there was no doubt about that. But old Mr. Bear, here, he really, really wanted it if you know what I mean.

Mr. Bear watched the bees come and go. He tried to figure out a time when the bees all left the hive, but they always kept guard. He pretended to sleep nearby, but Turtle noticed that he always kept one eye half open toward the beehive. Old Mr. Bear got grumpier and grumpier as he thought about the honey and waited for the right time.

The other animals watched old Mr. Bear thinking about that honey and plotting how to get it. They knew that there were other kinds of sweet things to get in the forest, like berries, sassafras roots, and sweet hickory nuts, so they went around having a good time feasting in the forest and putting up things for the winter.

Old Mr. Bear became so fixated on that hive of honey that he plumb forgot to start fattening up for the winter. He became so agitated about the honey that none of his friends could get near him to have a chat about winter coming, the weather changing, and such things.

But the bees were no dummies, and they were ready for him. There was no one in the forest who hadn't seen him thinking and plotting about that honey. Even the bees had heard the other animals gossiping.

"That old Mr. Bear has his mind so fixed on that honey that he's not even getting ready for winter. Too much thinking, I'd say," said Blue Jay. "We have to leave soon, and usually, by the time we leave, he's pretty fixed for winter, but not this year."

Everyone in the forest but Mr. Bear could see the kind of trouble his thinking was getting him into.

Finally, he had worked himself into such a frenzy with his thinking about that honey that he charged the tree and tried to grab the honeycomb.

The bees were ready for him. The foot soldiers crawled over him and stung him wherever they could. The queen's guard, the flying specialists, dive-bombed him and stung his eyes, mouth, and gums, and some even were willing to attack his tongue. It was a fierce battle.

Mr. Bear grabbed a little bit of honeycomb, but he was blind from the beestings, and his mouth and paws hurt so bad that he fell out of the tree and hit the ground with a huge thud. He was knocked out for sure.

The other animals cautiously gathered around. They loved Mr. Bear and knew that he was part of their family. Yet no one wanted to be around Mr. Bear when he was hurt or angry, so they just got into a big circle and waited.

Bobcat cautiously tried to lick his eyes a bit to heal them. Turtle slowly went to the creek and brought back some mud, and Raccoon patted it onto his eyes as a poultice to soothe the beestings. Even the bees brought little bits of honey, and the ants crawled into his mouth and deposited it on his stings, for they all knew that honey was good for healing stings too.

Most of the animals took a taste of the sweet honey that was scattered on the ground and in Mr. Bear's fur, for every one of them liked the sweet honey, but only Mr. Bear seemed greedy with it. The others seemed satisfied with what the bees dropped for them and the sweetness the flowers offered up before the bees got there. There was plenty to go around.

The dragonflies whispered to one another that it was a shame that Mr. Bear had thought and thought so much about that honey. They figured that all that thinking had made him a little crazy in the head.

The dragonflies buzzed around and talked with the other creatures of the forest, and they all agreed that they felt sorry for Mr. Bear and could see that all that thinking had sure enough caused great trouble for him.

They all agreed they liked Mr. Bear; he just lost himself when he thought too much about the honey.

Mr. and Mrs. Porcupine agreed to guard the honeycomb so Mr. Bear would have it when he woke up. The bees agreed they thought he had learned his lesson, and they could work harder and make more honey before winter. Some of the other animals agreed to gather extra food and share some of their winter stores with Mr. Bear. They knew that when he woke up, he would have a terrible headache from all that thinking, and he was sure to be hungry.

All the animals of the forest agreed to spend part of the day trying to help Mr. Bear. Anyone could get silly sometimes, and it was a good reminder of the kind of trouble that too much thinking could cause an otherwise good person.

All were happy that Mr. Bear was just knocked out and not dead. After all, they really liked him, and he was family.

# 6

# The Cat Who Lost His Purr

The family dragged themselves into their home after a long vacation.

Roddy's father brought him in from the car and carried him up to his room. Roddy's older sister, Elizabeth, grumbled as she too was shepherded up to bed. The family had been away on a long vacation, and everyone was very tired. No one had time to look around to find Tom, their big white cat with one bright yellow eye and one piercing blue eye.

Roddy slept late the next morning. When he came downstairs, his mother was already up, and the others had eaten breakfast and were off getting reacquainted with being home.

"Where's Tom?" Roddy said immediately.

"Tom's over there on the couch. Be careful with him. He's not well," his mother said.

"Not well?" Roddy said anxiously. "What's wrong with him?"

"I don't know," said Roddy's mother. "And he is old, you know."

Roddy tiptoed carefully over to Tom's side. He didn't want to disturb him or hurt him. Secretly, Tom was his best friend in the family, and Roddy loved him dearly. After all, it wasn't easy being the youngest member of this family, and Tom seemed to understand what it was like to be surrounded by older people, especially Roddy's older sister, who thought she was very sophisticated and knew everything.

In fact, there were many times when Tom was the only one who understood Roddy, and they would have long talks while Roddy petted Tom, with Tom keeping a steady stream of purrs to show that he understood Roddy completely.

Roddy went over to pet Tom. Tom allowed the petting, but there was no purr.

"Mommy, there's no purr," Roddy said, his voice almost reaching the level of the distress siren that sounded on the first day of every month to make sure it was working in case of an emergency.

"I know," his mother said with a soft sadness. "He seems to have lost his purr."

"Lost his purr?" Roddy wailed. "How can that be? Where did it go?"

"I don't know," his mother said. "Maybe the vet will know. I have made an appointment with him for Tom tomorrow. You can go with me if you want."

"Okay," said Roddy, "but this is an emergency. We have to find Tom's purr."

"Come eat your breakfast. I'm sure we'll find it," said his mother.

"I don't have time," said Roddy. "I have to do something."

"Roddy!" said his mother. "First, breakfast."

"Aw, okay," Roddy said, realizing his mother did not really understand how serious this purr thing was.

Roddy rushed through his breakfast, put his dishes in the sink so as not to cause another delay with his mother, and rushed outside.

First, he would go to Auntie Helen. Everyone always asked Auntie Helen about the really serious things, and Tom's purr was serious.

Auntie Helen was so glad to see him. She hugged him and wanted to hear about the trip. Roddy knew he must be respectful to elders, and Auntie Helen was really old, so he answered her questions, being as polite as he could be with the important problem he had.

He told her of their vacation: the desert; the big cactus plants with long, long stickers; a canyon called the Grand Canyon, which was even bigger than Waimea Canyon on their island; and the wild antelope he had seen.

"Did you like it?" she asked.

"Yes, but I have a big problem right now, and I wonder if you can help me."

"I'll try," Auntie Helen said.

"Auntie Helen, Tom has lost his purr. He always purrs. How will we talk if he has no purr?"

"Ah, this is serious," Auntie Helen said. "Why do you think Tom lost his purr?"

"I really don't care why," said Roddy, trying not to be impolite. "I just want to know where it is."

"Well, Roddy, I was just on my way to do my volunteer work at the church thrift shop. If you haven't found his purr by the time I get back, I'll help you look."

Roddy smiled inside. That was Auntie Helen—she always understood and would help.

"Why don't you go see Uncle Monty? He is always out working in his garden, and he may have seen Tom's purr wandering off."

"What a good idea!" Roddy exclaimed. "Uncle Monty is very, very old, but he's very wise, and he doesn't miss much, Mother always says."

"Your mother's right about that, I guess," exclaimed Auntie Helen.

Roddy dashed out the door and over to Uncle Monty's. Uncle Monty mostly spoke Japanese, but he understood almost everything Roddy said, and they were good friends. Everyone knew that.

Roddy saw Uncle Monty working in his garden. He waved when he saw Roddy and motioned him right over. Roddy did not want to be impolite, but he wanted to get right to the point since their conversations often took a long time with the Japanese talk and everything.

"Hi, Uncle Monty. I need your help. Tom has lost his purr, and I wonder if you have seen it or can help me find it."

Uncle Monty smiled. "This is serious," he said. "Let's look in my garden."

They looked around the squash and the peppers, under the beans on their tall poles, and alongside the bitter melons running over the ground. They looked under the grapefruit tree, and Uncle Monty gave Roddy a sack full of grapefruit for his family. There was no grapefruit in the world better than Uncle Monty's.

They looked under the house, in the shed, and down over the riverbank.

"I don't think it would have gone into the river since Tom doesn't go near the river," said Uncle Monty.

Roddy was relieved about that. If Tom's purr had gone into the river, there was no telling where it could have ended up. That was a terrible thought. All the little kids knew how dangerous the river could be for little ones.

Clearly, Tom's purr wasn't anywhere around Uncle Monty's.

"I'll go ask my friends for help," said Roddy. "Thank you for helping me, Uncle Monty. I'll let you know when I find it."

Uncle Monty smiled that knowing smile of his and waved as Roddy trotted off. Roddy knew Uncle Monty would keep looking and let him know if he found Tom's purr.

Next, Roddy went over to his friends' house. He knew they would understand and help. That was what friends did. Elders would always do what they could, and it was friends who would get down and dirty with you—he'd heard that expression from his older sister.

He slipped past the older kids. They were like his older sister. They always thought they were smarter, knew more, and "had all the answers," as his mother said, and they were lazy. Roddy needed real workers at this point, and his friends Kanani and Kauaihau were real workers.

Roddy slipped into their room, and they were so glad to see him. They started with a jumble of questions about his vacation. Roddy immediately shushed them, putting his finger up to his lips, and began to whisper.

"Tom has lost his purr, and he looks terrible. If we don't get his purr back, he may die."

His two friends looked stricken. "No can?" they said in the local pidgin dialect. They shook their heads, and all together they the three of them sneaked out of the house.

They spent hours looking for Tom's purr. They searched everywhere, but they couldn't find it. Roddy arrived back home sad, tired, and exhausted. He flopped down onto the couch. His mother was still busy getting the kitchen in order.

Tom, with great effort, painfully crawled into Roddy's lap. Slowly and quietly, he began to purr. Roddy petted him very gently and sat still, afraid to move. When his mother came over, tears were streaming down his cheeks.

His mother stopped and looked questioningly at Roddy.

Quietly, Roddy said, "I've found Tom's purr. I looked everywhere and couldn't find it. Then he and I found it together. It was hidden in my lap! Now that he's found his purr, he will get well." Roddy felt relief as he gently stroked Tom.

When he went to the vet with Tom and his mother the next day, Roddy listened quietly, holding Tom, as the grown-ups talked about medical things that didn't make much sense to him.

When the vet and his mother finished talking, Roddy looked up confidently and said, "He's going to get well. I know it because he and I found his purr. It was hiding in my lap, and he couldn't find it until I sat down and he crawled into my lap. Now he has it wherever he is, and he can get well."

Roddy's mother and the vet looked at one another knowingly, and the vet said, "I'm sure that's very true, Roddy."

And it was, just as Roddy had said.

7

# Spirit Horse: An Old-Fashioned Christmas

Dedicated to my grandson
Alexander Eusavio Saavedra


## A Historical Note

On August 3, 1956, a predominantly white male Congress, in its infinite wisdom, passed the Indian Relocation Act of 1956. Ostensibly, the purpose of the act was to "assimilate the first people of this nation into what had become the 'dominant culture.'" This great so-called "assimilation" was to be accomplished by relocating native people to the cities from their lands, their culture, and their time-tested wisdom, taking them away from their ancestors, their beliefs, and one another. Functionally, this "assimilation" almost resulted in a decimation of individuals, their accumulated wisdom, and an entire culture.

Unfortunately, it has taken us a very long time to realize that in the very purpose of the wisdom that can be the United States of America is that we need these mixtures of cultural wisdoms to help us be more whole as a species, as a nation, and as a planet.

Indeed, this shared wisdom might just be what ultimately will save us as a species and as a planet. It is our differences that are our greatest treasures and resources.

"Spirit Horse" helps us remember what we know.

# Chapter 1

Tommy's parents were sitting at the kitchen table, looking very sad. Tommy's dad had been sick and unable to work for many months and was feeling bad about not having any extra money for Christmas presents.

"With the money we have now, we just have enough to pay the rent and put food on the table. I'm afraid this will be a difficult Christmas for Tommy. Tommy was expecting a bike like all his ten-year-old friends, but he won't be getting it," said his father.

"I feel sad too that we don't have much money this year," his mother agreed. "It has been a difficult year for us all, and I'm sure Tommy will understand if we talk to him. He's a good boy, and even though he will be disappointed, he knows that the most important thing is that you are getting well."

"I know. I just wish I hadn't gotten sick," said his father.

"There will be other Christmases. Now, let's go to bed," his mother said gently.

Tommy's parents didn't know he was listening outside the door. He was so excited about Christmas that he couldn't sleep. He had been heading for the kitchen, when he'd heard them talking.

Tommy was glad he had not walked in or let them know he was there. They felt bad enough. At least he knew now that he would not be getting a big red bicycle, as the other boys would.

*After all, I don't want to be selfish. Dad's getting well is the most important thing,* he thought with tears of disappointment running down his cheeks.

Tommy ran to his room, flung himself onto his bed, and cried himself to sleep.

As he slept, a soft, wispy gray mist began to rise over his bed. Almost magically, the mist formed into an old Indian chief in full headdress and beautifully beaded buckskin clothes. He was so old that his face was layered in wrinkles. Even though he was old, his eyes were clear as they looked down on Tommy with love and concern. Soon a lovely old woman dressed in a beaded buckskin dress, leggings, and moccasins began to appear at the old man's side. She had long gray braids, and her face was gentle and loving. Slowly, others appeared, until ten of Tommy's ancestors were lovingly gathered around his bed. The Ancient Ones had arrived.

"Our great-great-great-great-grandson Tommy needs our help," said the old chief in a concerned and clear voice. "He has lived in the city, far from his land and his people, and he feels alone."

"Our people have endured much, but we have always had one another, and we know our place with the land, which has made the pain bearable," said another.

"Tommy and his family are isolated and alone. This makes difficulties much harder to bear," said a strong young warrior at Tommy's feet.

"Tommy's pain is deeper than not getting the bicycle," said a beautiful young woman in a quilled buckskin dress at Tommy's side. "We need to do the work of the ancestors and give Tommy what he needs: his roots and the knowledge of his people."

"Yes, Tommy is our seventh generation, and we have planned and lived our lives always thinking of those who come after us," said the old chief. He turned to the young Indian boy at his side. "Running Bear, will you be Tommy's companion and help bring him to the gifts we are going to give him this holiday season?"

"I would be honored, Grandfather," the boy said respectfully, looking lovingly at the old man.

"First, we must see that Tommy has a spirit horse. The horse will take him back in time to the land of his people. Tommy must know that he is part of a great and proud people, a people who live with the Great Spirit and are one with all creation," said the chief. "We will go now, and tomorrow night we will return."

# Chapter 2

Tommy awoke the next morning feeling strangely at peace with himself. When he thought about it, he felt sad that he would not get his red bicycle for Christmas, but at least he had a week to get used to the idea.

School seemed easy that day, even though there was a lot of excitement about the school holidays coming up. All the kids were talking about Christmas and what they were getting. Tommy tried to avoid those discussions. He was eager to get home that evening. At least there were only four more days of school left before school vacation. It would be easier when school was out.

After dinner, Tommy seemed restless. He couldn't get interested in anything. Finally, he came into the kitchen, where his parents were talking.

"I'm tired. I think I'll go to bed," Tommy said. His parents felt concerned as they looked at one another and then at Tommy.

"You aren't sick, are you?" said his father.

"Come here, and let me feel your forehead," his mother said, stretching out her hand. "No fever. You sure you're okay?"

"I'm sure," Tommy said. He hugged his mother and father and kissed them both good night.

Tommy wasn't quite sure why he wanted to go to bed so early; it just seemed like a nice, quiet place to be, and he wanted to be alone for a while. Soon he drifted off to sleep, and immediately, his new friends, the ancestors, began to emerge over his bed.

This time, the young boy, Running Bear, was astride a beautiful blood bay horse with a black mane and tail. He looked powerful and important as he sat on his magnificent steed.

In his hand, Running Bear held a braided rawhide lead rope for a lovely brown-and-white paint mare. Her head was all brown, with a wide white blaze running from her forelock down over her nose. Her forelock was white like her mane and hung long into her blaze. It quivered with the breeze as she tossed her head. Her body was brown, with large dollops of white, and her tail was white like her mane and forelock. She had three white socks. The hooves on the legs with the white socks were white, and the hoof on the brown leg was black. She was beyond beautiful! Her head was up, and her ears were pushed forward. Her eyes sparkled like a deep pool in the river, and she was prancing and pawing the air in anticipation. She seemed ready for something.

The old grandfather chief looked down on Tommy. His smile was warm, his eyes were gentle, and he seemed to have in him the love of centuries of his people.

"Tommy, we have come to take you with us tonight. We do not call you Tommy. To us, you are known as Returning Boy. This is the name we have given you from our people, because in your pain, we came. You have returned.

"Running Bear is holding your horse for you. This is your spirit horse. This horse will take you back to your land, back to your people. Your spirit horse will always be with you, even when you are awake and can't see her. She will always bring you back to your land and to your people."

Tommy—Returning Boy—suddenly found himself standing by his horse with his ancestors gathered around him. Tentatively, he reached out and touched Spirit Horse's beautiful spotted body. He could feel the life and excitement in her, and he felt the same feelings come through his fingers. It was as if he and his horse were connected by an invisible current. He looked up and saw Running Bear smiling down at him.

"Are you ready to go?" Running Bear asked.

Returning Boy nodded vigorously. "Yes."

"Then hop on, and let's go, my brother," Running Bear said as he moved out on his horse.

Returning Boy grabbed the braided reins and hopped onto the bare back of Spirit Horse. She was ready, and off they went behind Running Bear.

*Ta-tacka, ta-tacka, ta-tacka.* They galloped into the mist.

Suddenly, they were in the country. The land was beautiful! The prairie grass was so tall it reached up under Spirit Horse's belly. The grasses waved for miles and miles. A clear stream flowed from the mountains, with majestic cottonwoods lining its banks.

A doe and a fawn stood by the stream, carefully looking at the two horses and riders. Returning Boy had never seen anything so beautiful in his life.

The earth was so green, the sky was so blue, and the stream was so clear. Returning Boy was so overwhelmed he could hardly speak.

"It's so beautiful!" he said, his eyes getting misty.

"Yes, Returning Boy. This is your home. This is the land of your people. Your ancestors are buried here, and the ancestors of your ancestors are buried here. Your roots, like the roots of those trees, go deep here. It is sad when people do not know their land. They can never feel secure unless they know their place with their land and their people."

Returning Boy felt his eyes fill with tears, as he knew that he did indeed belong to this place. He had never felt anything so intensely in his life.

He was concerned that he might be embarrassed or embarrass Running Bear, but when he looked at Running Bear, he could see that he had tears in his eyes too.

"The land is our grandmother and our mother," said Running Bear. "She provides for all our needs. She gives us our food. She gives us our shelter. She gives us our life. When we are confused or alone, we have only to return to the breast of our mother, the earth, and she will heal us. We love and respect our Mother Earth. We must never forget that we are one with our mother, and when we care for her, we care for ourselves. Without the earth and the streams, we are nothing."

Returning Boy had never heard these things before, yet he knew their truth deep inside himself.

"Remember, Returning Boy, this is your land and the land of your people. You are always a child of our mother, the earth."

Returning Boy felt the strength of Spirit Horse between his legs. He was aware of her hooves upon their mother, the earth. He could feel the strength of the earth flow up through Spirit Horse's legs into his own body and back down again into the earth. He *felt* his oneness with the earth. He was not separate. He was not alone. He would never be alone again, because he was one with all of nature.

Running Bear looked at Returning Boy and knew that Returning Boy had learned a lesson this night that would never leave him. Gently, he said, "Returning Boy, it's time to go back for now. We can come back again tomorrow night if you wish."

Returning Boy hated to leave that beautiful place. Still, he knew inside that he could indeed return any time he wanted or needed to. He had his spirit horse.

# Chapter 3

Tommy awoke the next day feeling even better than the day before. All day long, he had the feeling that there was something he wanted to remember, and he almost remembered it but not quite.

"Never mind," he said to himself. "It will come to me."

That night, again, going to bed was easy, and Tommy seemed happy. His parents felt relieved to see him so happy.

As soon as Tommy fell asleep, he saw Running Bear seated on his big bay horse, holding the reins of Spirit Horse. They were waiting for him.

Tommy called out, "Hi, Running Bear! Where are the others?" as he jumped onto Spirit Horse.

"They are waiting for us back at camp. I'll race you!" Running Bear shouted, digging his heels into his horse's sides.

"Yeehaw!" Returning Boy yelled as he leaned down on Spirit Horse's withers and urged her on. He felt as if he had been riding this little paint horse all his life. Yet he had never even been on a horse until the night before.

The two of them came riding up to the camp like wild animals, but they pulled up short just as they reached the edge of the camp. They did not want to frighten the little children who were playing in and among the lodges. They knew that big boys like them who were old enough to have horses must take care of the little ones and look out for them. Returning Boy felt proud that everyone in his tribe was important, and each had responsibilities. Running Bear had told him, "All people contribute what they can to the good of the tribe, and everyone is taken care of. If someone gets sick and cannot hunt, food is shared with his family, just like all the hunters share food with Grandfather and Grandmother since they have become too old to hunt."

Returning Boy thought, *How much easier it would have been on my father if he had been among his people when he got sick.*

"Are the old chief and the old woman really your grandparents?" he asked.

"They are everybody's grandparents. We all have many grandparents, just as we have many brothers and sisters. Nobody 'owns' anyone else. We share grandparents. All wise ones are grandfather or grandmother or sometimes auntie or uncle, but all of them are our teachers. It is a privilege to be able to sit and listen to what the old ones have to teach us. They have lived the longest. They are the best teachers," said Running Bear.

*My teachers at school are young,* thought Returning Boy. *And I have to leave home to learn. How different it is to be taught by the old ones and to be taught as life unfolds.*

As Returning Boy walked through the village, leading Spirit Horse, everyone waved and called to him. The little ones ran up and asked if they could pat Spirit Horse on the nose. Returning Boy indeed felt he was returning home, and everyone knew him. He was proud to have such a fine horse as Spirit Horse.

The camp was on the edge of the beautiful stream Returning Boy had seen the day before. He had never seen the sky so blue. The stream and the sky seemed to be one.

Returning Boy saw the old chief seated on the ground beside the door to his lodge. Some of the children were sitting around him, listening.

"The sky is our grandfather. Without Grandfather Sky, Grandmother Earth could not feed, clothe, and take care of us. Grandfather Sky gives us the sun to heat our days. Without the sun, the plants would not grow, and without the plants, all the animals, including us, would have nothing to eat. The plants feed the birds of the air, the winged; the bugs, the crawling; the animals, the four-leggeds; and the fish, the swimming. The four-footed and the two-footed are all our brothers and sisters, and the Creator has given us to one another. We all share in the gifts of the Creator. Everyone and everything, no matter who we are or what we are, all have the same mother and the same father. Even people who are not like us have the same mother and the same father. All people are our brothers and sisters."

The old chief looked tenderly at the children seated around him. His voice was deep and resonant and had the scratchiness of a voice long used in teaching his people. He never tired of sharing his stories with his children, and the children of the camp never tired of hearing his stories.

The children knew that the elders had lived longer than anyone, gathering wisdom all along their journey through life. It was a privilege to listen to them and to hear their stories. Listening to their stories was the way the children learned to become part of the tribe. Each child there, with shining eyes and ears grown big from listening, would be expected to tell those same stories and be grandfather or grandmother to the future generations as they came along.

Returning Boy and Running Bear had quietly moved to the edge of the group and joined the other children.

"The sky also brings us the rain and the snow, which bathe Grandmother Earth and nourish each growing new life. We welcome the rain and the snow, just as we welcome the sunshine. Without all of them, there would be no life on this planet.

"From the sky come the lightning and the Thunder Beings, who bring magic to us. The sky also is the home of the eagle. The eagle is the protector of the earth. The eagle flies higher than any other bird, and it has very keen sight. The eagle flies so high that it can see the whole picture. The sky holds the eagle so it can give us perspective and vision. Without the eagle, our sight is limited."

Grandfather smiled at the children. He was glad to see that Returning Boy and Running Bear had joined them for storytime. He knew that these stories were what Returning Boy needed to know—stories about who he was, his land, and his people.

The old chief also knew that Returning Boy's mother and father needed to hear these stories as much as Returning Boy did. Knowing that they belonged to an ancient tradition that had been alive for centuries and would be alive for centuries to come would heal them of their loneliness and isolation. Returning Boy could bring these gifts to his parents if he could but remember them when he awakened.

The old chief looked at Returning Boy and Running Bear. Then he said gently, "You two had better get Returning Boy back for tonight. The sun will rise soon and fulfill the Creator's promise of a new day."

Running Bear and Returning Boy ran and jumped onto their horses and headed back. Both of their horses loved these races back to today. They ran like the wind with tails flying and ears flat against their heads.

"Night," said Returning Boy.

"G'night," said Running Bear. "I'll be here tomorrow."

"I'll be waiting for you," said Returning Boy as he settled into his "real" self, Tommy.

# Chapter 4

"Good morning, Mom. Good morning, Dad," Tommy said as he breezed into the kitchen. "Only two more days before school vacation."

Tommy's mother and father knew that meant Christmas was close at hand. They were dreading Christmas. They had been able to buy Tommy some bright striped socks. He would like the colors, and he needed them, and that day, his mother was going to get him a new pair of jeans, which he desperately needed. At least he would have two gifts to open on Christmas Day. They had decided it was more important to get something for Tommy than to get something for each other. They could get what they needed after Dad went back to work.

Tommy ate a quick breakfast and rushed off to school.

"Does he seem different to you?" his mother said to his father.

"I dunno. Maybe it's all the excitement about Christmas," his dad said.

"Maybe," said his mother.

The day at school again went quickly. Tommy seemed distracted, but he didn't cause trouble. That was good.

Again, that night, there was no fuss about going to bed. His parents noticed that Tommy seemed different about going to bed, but they were tired and somewhat depressed about the fast approach of Christmas, so they didn't say anything.

Tommy fell asleep immediately. Running Bear was waiting for him with their horses. Returning Boy jumped onto Spirit Horse, and off they went.

"Grandfather suggested that we don't even need to come into the camp this time. We can just take a ride across the land the Creator has provided for us," Running Bear said.

"That's great," said Returning Boy. "Let's ride out on the prairie."

They turned their horses to the east, away from the mountains, and eased into a slow canter. Returning Boy was again aware of his oneness with Spirit Horse and how much he loved her. There were times when she moved so effortlessly in her canter that he lost awareness of being on her. It was as if the two of them were one and moving as one across the land. There was no need to pay attention to his riding, because he wasn't riding; he was moving with Spirit Horse. At those times, even when she shied from a bush or a sudden rising bird, Returning Boy did not have to hold on or even tighten his knees. He and Spirit Horse sidestepped together and came back to the trail together. He knew he could never have that kind of intimacy with a bicycle.

As they came over a small rise, both horses stopped short. In front of them was a moving sea of brown—a huge herd of grazing buffalo. The herd seemed to stretch on for miles. Returning Boy had never seen anything like it. Spirit Horse was trembling, and she snorted as she tossed her head. Returning Boy could feel her tension and excitement.

"The buffalo are a gift from Wakan Tanka, the Creator," said Running Bear. "They provide for many of our needs. They give us food; the blanket robes for our beds; the skins for our lodges; hooves for our rattles; and bones for eating, making utensils, and decoration. We use every part of the buffalo. We do not waste anything. It would not be respectful to the Creator or to the buffalo to waste anything. We thank the buffalo for giving its life for us, and we give prayers and offerings for its generosity.

"Also, we never take more than we need. It is an insult to the Creator to hoard or take more than we need. We believe that if we live in balance with all of creation, our needs will be met. It is only when one group takes more than it needs or wastes what it has, that the balance is disturbed, and all will not have what they need."

Returning Boy pondered the words of Running Bear. *Do I really need a bicycle?* he thought. *How much waste there is in the world around me! What if we all stopped wasting? Would there be enough for everybody then?*

"We must remember that we share this land with the buffalo and all of Wakan Tanka's creation. We have no greater right to it than the buffalo, the birds, or the moles who live in it. We live together here," said Running Bear.

"How different this is from where I live!" said Returning Boy. "We hardly ever even see the earth. Our playground is covered with concrete. The only time we ever really see birds is on school field trips to the museum, and then they are dead and stuffed."

Running Bear looked at Returning Boy in shock and horror. "You must be awfully lonely," he said quietly, diverting his eyes.

"I am," whispered Returning Boy.

That moment hung suspended in the air around them. Neither knew what to say next. Then Spirit Horse snorted and tossed her head, breaking the spell.

"Let's ride back toward the hills," said Running Bear.

They moved down the knoll in a slow walk. As they went along, Running Bear pointed out various plants and told Returning Boy their uses.

"See those there? Those are wild turnips. The women dig them and make a wonderful stew with buffalo meat. They are always careful not to take them all. They leave a few that can go to seed so we will have more next year. It is important to respect each plant and leave enough so it can continue to seed and grow. If we take care of it that way, it will take care of us."

Running Bear pointed to a bush beside the path. "See that little bush? We dig the roots and use some of the bark to make a tea. We drink the tea in the spring. It helps clean the blood and gets us ready for spring and summer. Grandmother says it thins the blood and gets us ready for the warm weather.

"That plant over there—the one with the white blossoms—we use that for poultices. We gather the flowers, heat them, and mash them up. Then, while the blossoms are still warm, we make a pack and put it on infected places. The poultice pulls the infection out and gets poisons out of the blood so the wound can heal."

"Does everything have a use?" asked Returning Boy.

"Yes," said Running Bear. "Everything has its place in the plan of the Creator. We are only one part of the creation."

"But this is all *free?*" Returning Boy said it as a statement and a question.

"Yes," said Running Bear. "The Creator has provided for our needs and the needs of our brothers and sisters, the animals, birds, fish, and crawling things. It is all here."

"Just think," said Returning Boy. "If my father had been here, this medicine might have helped him. He and my mother might not have had to be so worried about money."

"That may be true," said Running Bear thoughtfully.

"There is so much," said Returning Boy. "So much to see, so much to learn, so much to experience—so much."

"Yes, there is!" said Running Bear, breaking into a big grin. "And only so much time. I'll get into big trouble if I don't get you back in time," he said as he tightened his legs around his big bay, urging him into a fast canter.

Spirit Horse followed suit, and they were soon back to their meeting place.

Returning Boy looked at Running Bear. "I can't tell you how much all this means to me."

"You don't have to," said Running Bear. "Grandfather knew it would. You called to us over the centuries, and answering that call is one of the greatest honors we ever have. I am honored to have this time with you. I'll be here tomorrow and whenever you need me."

Returning Boy slid off Spirit Horse. She nuzzled him in the shoulder as he looked up at Running Bear. He could feel her warm breath on his back, and he knew, indeed, that he would never be without her.

# Chapter 5

When Tommy got to school on the last day before vacation, he knew exactly what he wanted to do. He went to his teacher, Miss Clark. Miss Clark was a nice woman, probably in her midtwenties. She tried hard to teach them, and as he looked at her, Tommy realized that he and his friends didn't help her much. They were not very eager learners. Of course, learning from books about things that didn't seem to matter much was not as much fun as listening to Grandfather, Tommy realized.

*I'll have to be nicer to Miss Clark*, he thought as he approached her desk.

"Miss Clark, I was wondering if it would be all right with you if I could take some paper and paints home to work with over school break."

Miss Clark knew that Tommy and his family had very little money. In fact, she had quietly submitted their names for a Christmas basket and some toys to be given by the fire department to children who would not be getting anything for Christmas. She knew it wouldn't be the bike that she guessed Tommy hoped for, and at least it would be something. The food baskets usually had a turkey or a ham, so his family could have a Christmas dinner.

Tommy came from a fiercely proud family. Miss Clark knew it might be hard for them to accept charity, and she also knew that Tommy's parents loved him and wanted the best for him; still, she knew accepting the Christmas basket would be difficult.

Tommy had shown some talent in art, and Miss Clark wanted to support that. *After all, if Tommy were in school, he would use the paints and the colors. What's the difference in his taking them home and working on something?* Miss Clark had already made her decision.

"I think it would be all right, Tommy. What are you going to do with them?" asked Miss Clark.

"It's a surprise," said Tommy.

Miss Clark could see that he was getting a little nervous. "That's okay, Tommy. I don't need to know what you are planning. You can show it to me after school break if you want. That's up to you. Go ahead and pick out the colors and paints you want."

Tommy quickly chose a wide range of paints, knowing he could mix new colors at home too. He chose a variety of colored papers and large sheets of white paper.

Miss Clark produced a shopping bag to put it all in. "It looks like it's going to be a big project, Tommy."

"It is!" he said as he dashed out the door.

Since it was a short day at school, Tommy arrived home early. His mother and dad were not around, so he quickly scurried to his room and put his art supplies under his bed. He pulled out a big felt-tipped pen and began writing on one of the large pieces of white paper folded in fourths.

He was so involved in his work he had no idea how long he had been at it, when he heard the front door open and his mother's voice call out, "Tommy, we're home! Are you home yet?"

"I'm in here," Tommy said, quickly gathering up his materials and putting them under his bed. He rushed out to meet his parents. He surely didn't want them snooping around his room. Not that they ever did—he just didn't want to arouse their suspicion.

"I had to take your father to the doctor today. The doctor thinks he may be able to go back to work after the New Year," his mother said.

"That's great!" Tommy said, hoping the news would cheer up his father. He always seemed to look so sad. *I guess sitting in a wheelchair all these months would make anyone sad*, thought Tommy.

"I think I will go outside to play a little," Tommy told his mother.

"Be sure to get back before dark," she answered.

Tommy went outside. The world there was so gray and cold. The sky was a leaden gray, and the air was heavy. The buildings were gray, the concrete streets and sidewalks were gray, and there seemed to be a lifelessness around him. *At least I have my land*, thought Tommy. *I hope we have some snow for Christmas. Snow would clean and nourish the land.*

"Hey, Tommy, want to play some kickball?" his friends yelled.

"Sure," Tommy said as he ran to meet them.

In a little while, it started to get dark, and all the kids headed home.

Good smells were coming out of the kitchen, and Tommy thought of wild turnip and buffalo stew. *It must taste wonderful!*

After dinner and cleanup, they all sat around the table and talked. They talked about family and other Christmases. No one said it, but there in the city, they felt so far from their family. They knew a few other families at the Indian center, but they hadn't been there much since Dad got sick.

"Well, I think I'll go to my room. Miss Clark gave me a project to work on, and I want to finish it before Christmas." That wasn't quite the truth, but it wasn't a lie either, and Tommy knew that this kind of teasing "not-quite-truth" was acceptable around Christmastime. "Good night."

"Good night, Tommy," said his parents, still a little worried.

Tommy closed his door and brought out his art materials. He wrote, cut, pasted, colored, arranged, and rearranged. He worked until he was pleased with what he saw. Again, the time slipped by fast. Finally, he put away the supplies and fell into bed.

Sleep came like a soft blanket covering his being. Soon he was walking to meet Running Bear and Spirit Horse. Spirit Horse nickered, and as he approached her, Returning Boy grabbed a handful of grass to give her. She took the grass and nuzzled his chest.

"Looks like she knows whose horse she is," Running Bear said, laughing.

"I think we kinda belong to each other," Returning Boy said, putting his arm over Spirit Horse's neck and patting her. "What are we doing today?" he asked.

"Grandfather thought it would be wise to learn about the animals," Running Bear answered.

"Great!" said Returning Boy, jumping onto Spirit Horse.

They headed for their land at a gentle lope. "Maybe this is a good place to start," said Running Bear, pulling up his big bay.

Returning Boy looked around and couldn't see any animals at all. How could they learn about the animals if there weren't any? Or maybe Running Bear was just going to talk about them, like Miss Clark did.

Running Bear slid off his horse, and Returning Boy joined him.

"What are we going to do? Where are the animals? I don't see any animals around here. How can we learn about animals if there are none? What kind of animals does Grandfather want me to learn about?" Returning Boy was full of questions. It was good to ask questions in school. Miss Clark liked that.

"Just sit down, and be quiet," Running Bear said. "Grandfather says we can't learn when we are asking questions."

They both sat down in the tall grass. Their horses, with their braided rawhide reins dragging on the ground, grazed nearby.

Returning Boy was getting restless. If he was supposed to be learning about animals, why weren't they *doing* something? He glanced over at Running Bear, who was just sitting there, doing nothing.

Returning Boy began to fidget. He couldn't seem to get comfortable. Running Bear didn't say anything. He just sat quietly.

Finally, Returning Boy quieted down. Slowly, he noticed that there were ants running back and forth in a path just beyond his crossed feet. Running Bear was watching them too. They seemed *busy*, and they seemed to know just where they were going. Some were carrying heavy loads on their backs. Returning Boy put a small piece of dirt in their path, and *they moved it*. He was amazed at the strength they had when they worked together. They could move things much bigger than they were. When one ant tried to move it, nothing happened. Then that ant seemed to "talk with" another ant, and suddenly, there were a whole bunch of ants around the piece of dirt, and *they moved it out of their path*. Returning Boy was impressed.

"Did you see that? Boy, are they strong! They just kept at it until they moved that dirt!" Returning Boy exclaimed, his eyes wide in wonder.

"The ants have much to teach us about community. They know a lot about working together. Also, they are patient. They don't have to accomplish everything right away.

They plan, they wait, they get who and what they need to do the job, and then they do the job," said Running Bear.

"Wow, I didn't realize ants were so intelligent," Returning Boy said.

"They have a lot to teach us if we are willing to just stop to take the time to listen," said Running Bear. "They are always there to teach. We just have to stop, be quiet, and be ready to learn."

Returning Boy realized that he didn't stop to listen very often and that he had not been taught to learn by stopping, and listening, and watching. He had always thought one learned by asking questions.

Just as he was thinking about this, a field mouse ran by. He caught a glimpse of her out of the corner of his eye—just a motion, and then she was gone. Returning Boy sat very, very still. Soon the mouse scurried back to where she had come from. She disappeared down a tiny hole.

Returning Boy and Running Bear held their breath and waited. Soon her wee head poked out of her hole. She looked cautiously from side to side, and then out she came again, and she rushed off. When she returned, Returning Boy noticed that she had something in her mouth. With her eyes darting here and there, she scurried to her hole. Returning Boy was impressed with how cautious and careful she was while still keeping very busy.

The two boys watched her for a long time. Returning Boy became so fascinated with her comings and goings that he lost all track of time. Only when Running Bear threw a little stone at him did he take his eyes off the mouse. Running Bear signaled that they should go. Returning Boy had been sitting still for so long that when he tried to stand up, his legs buckled, and he tumbled to the ground. Running Bear rushed over to him and offered his hand to his friend to help him up, but Returning Boy pulled on him, and they both rolled around on the ground, laughing.

"We'd better get back," said Running Bear. "We've been here a long time."

"We have?" said Returning Boy. "I guess I got completely focused on the mouse. She was so busy and so cautious and so careful. I never realized that mice were so orderly and careful."

"Yes, we have a lot to learn from her. You're right; they *are* very careful and orderly," said Running Bear.

When they reached their meeting place, Returning Boy slid off Spirit Horse and took her head in his arms. He really loved this horse!

"Time to go," said Running Bear.

"I know," Returning Boy answered reluctantly. "I'll see you tomorrow."

# Chapter 6

Tommy spent all Christmas Eve working in his room. His mother had tried to cheer up the apartment with decorations they had saved over the years. Although they all knew that this would be a bleak Christmas, there was an air of excitement and anticipation in the apartment that day.

That night at dinner, Tommy's father paused before they ate and said, "Let's stop and thank the Creator for all we have."

Tommy was surprised because he had not heard his parents pray in a long time. He felt warm inside when his father said they needed to thank the Creator. Grandfather and his people prayed all the time, and in the time Tommy had spent with his people, prayer had become natural to him.

The food basket and a baseball and bat had arrived from the firemen that day while Tommy was working in his room. At first, Tommy's dad felt proud and didn't want to accept the gifts. Then a gentle touch on his arm caused him to turn and look at Tommy's mother. He could see so much in her eyes—so much suffering, so much concern, so much love—and he realized that his family's joy and comfort for the holiday were more important than his pride.

Tommy's father had become confused while living there in the city. On his land and with his people, he was a proud person because of who he was and who his ancestors were. There in the city, he was valued only for what he did and how much money he had, and he hadn't been able to be a person who would make Tommy proud. Yet he knew that his love for Tommy was much more important than his pride.

That night, he felt grateful for the gifts of food and toys, and he remembered that all people were his brothers and sisters and that all gifts came from the Creator.

"Let's thank the Creator for the many gifts we have been given: the earth, the skies, and all our relations. Let's be grateful that we have food on our table and that we have each other. *Mitakuye oyasin.* We pray for all our relations."

Tommy had tears in his eyes as he looked up after the prayer. He had the feeling he was back with Grandfather. "What's mitakuye oy—whatever it is?" he asked.

"Mitakuye oyasin. In our language, that means 'all our relations'—not just our immediate family, like us here, or just our people. When we pray, we pray for all our relations—all Indian people, all black people, all yellow people, and all white people. We always pray for all our brothers and sisters all over the world. And we also pray for all our other brothers and sisters among the animals, the birds, the crawling, the swimming, and all creation. This helps us remember that we are connected to all creation and a part of all creation. It's good to remember that."

Tommy felt as if he were listening to Grandfather speak. He was proud of his father.

After dinner, Tommy went to his room to finish his project.

When he had everything just as he wanted it, he cleaned up his mess and hid his project under his bed. He had gathered some newspapers and painted lovely pictures on them to use for wrapping paper. He had left one page blank to fill in after his visit with his people that night.

As he drifted off to sleep, Tommy could almost hear Spirit Horse nickering to him—and indeed, she was! She was clearly as eager to see Returning Boy as he was to see her. Running Bear no longer held her lead rope, and when she saw Returning Boy, she trotted up, nuzzled him in the chest, and nickered softly. Returning Boy held her head close to his chest and buried his face in her forelock. He really loved his horse!

He then looked up at Running Bear and said, "Well, what's for tonight, my friend?" As he said the words, both boys knew that Running Bear was truly his friend.

"Grandfather wants us to come to the camp. This is your last night before the Christmas holiday," Running Bear told him.

"I know," said Returning Boy, glancing down.

"But you can return to us anytime you want," Running Bear added hastily, and they both grinned.

Returning Boy swung up onto Spirit Horse, and they moved off toward the camp in a gentle lope.

Grandfather was waiting for them, as were all the other members of the camp. The little ones were excited, ducking in and out between the legs of the adults as they stood around quietly talking in small groups. There was an air of festivity in the camp, and the smells that wafted through the camp made Returning Boy's mouth water.

When he and Running Bear arrived, they left their ponies at the edge of camp and began moving toward Grandfather's lodge. Returning Boy felt his place in this wave of people. He knew he would always have his place.

"Returning Boy, this is a special night where you live. It is the night before the birth of a great man, a great teacher. We honor all people and all religions. Our concern is not how a person prays—that is up to each person. Our concern is *that* they pray. When a man, woman, or child prays, no matter how he or she does it, we always stand beside that person as his or her relative. We are all part of the Great Spirit and, therefore, brothers and sisters. All of us as a people have been given a way that is unique to us to approach the Great Spirit. None is better than any other. We respect all approaches to the Great Spirit.

"Returning Boy, tonight I want to teach you about the medicine wheel. The medicine wheel is central to our entire way of life.

"You will notice that everything in nature is in a circle. Birds build their nests in circles. Wasps build their nests in circles. The sun travels from east to west and around from east to west again. Our lodges are circular, and we place them in a circle. Our medicine wheel is a circle. We have the four directions: east, south, west, and north.

"Of these four directions, the east is the place of the rising sun. It is the land of the red people, our people. It is from the east that the Great Spirit fulfills the promise of a new day. It is good every morning to get up, say prayers, and greet the sunrise.

"When we think of the south, we think of yellow, and it reminds us of our brothers and sisters the yellow people. From the south comes the warm sun and the heat that helps Grandmother Earth grow all her abundant life.

"The west is the direction of the black people and the Thunder Beings, who bring us rain to wash the earth and water for our streams and lakes.

"The north is the direction of our white brothers and sisters. From the north come the snows of winter, which water the earth and give us a time of quiet to rest in our lodges and tell the legends and stories of our people.

"The four directions tell us of our four seasons—spring, summer, fall, and winter—and they help us remember that life is a cycle, and living is a cycle.

"The medicine wheel reminds us that we humans also live in a cycle, like the seasons. Our life is a cycle—the baby, the youth, the adult, and the elder. All cycles are important, and death is not to be feared. Death is only part of the cycle.

"So you see, Returning Boy, the medicine wheel is basic to all our teachings. There is always more to learn about the medicine wheel."

Returning Boy tried hard to remember everything that Grandfather had said. He knew that these were important teachings and that someday he would be responsible for teaching them to his children and grandchildren. He also knew he would have many more chances to learn about the medicine wheel. He could not learn all of it at once. The teachings needed to sink in.

"Thank you, Grandfather. I will hold these teachings close to my heart and share them when it is time," said Returning Boy. He felt humble in Grandfather's presence.

"You are welcome, my grandson," said the old chief. He reached out and laid his hand on Returning Boy's head, and Returning Boy was aware that he was receiving a powerful blessing.

Grandfather continued. "Before you return this night, I want to do two more things. First, we have prepared a proper naming ceremony for you. It is important that you have your full name and a ceremony wherein this name is given to you. Next, the camp has prepared a feast for you on this special occasion."

Then he spoke to the people of his village. "We shall prepare the ceremony." Several people came forward with fresh-cut sage and covered the ground in front of the old chief with it. Others brought forward four flags in the colors of the medicine wheel: red, yellow, black, and white. The four flags were on short sticks and were placed at the edge of the carpet of sage in the four directions: red toward the east, yellow toward the south, black toward the west, and white toward the north.

"Returning Boy, will you stand in the middle of the sage and face the east?" asked Grandfather. "I will be behind you."

Returning Boy moved to the center of the sage and faced east. He felt secure in knowing Grandfather was behind him. Running Bear and three other young men came forward. Each held a string with little bundles tied to it.

"These are tobacco bundles. They have been tied as offerings in your honor. They will be wrapped around the four flags for the four directions and enclose you in the circle. All life is a circle, and you will be in the center of the circle of life," Grandfather said.

Returning Boy moved to the center of the circle, and as he did so, he saw that Grandfather had tied a black cloth bandanna over his eyes.

The drum started beating, and Grandfather's voice rose high over the people as he began the ceremony. Returning Boy clasped his hands together as they hung in front of him, and he lowered his head.

As Grandfather continued to chant and sing, Returning Boy lost all sense of time and space. It was now, and it was forever, all at the same time. Nothing really mattered but Grandfather's voice. Returning Boy was very sure the Creator was speaking through Grandfather's voice. The language was the old language of his people. Returning Boy could not understand it with his mind, but his heart heard and understood every word.

Returning Boy felt as if he were taken to some other time and place. He seemed to be in all time and all places. The drum and the voice soared up through the clouds, over the mountains, over the streams, and across the oceans to all peoples in all lands. Returning Boy joined the eagle and could see all lands and all peoples. He saw all life.

As Grandfather's voice and the drum stopped, Returning Boy felt himself return to himself and his place on the sage. He looked up. The entire camp was gathered in a semicircle, facing him. They were all looking at him with love in their eyes. Even the children, who usually were running around with great energy, were quietly standing there. This was a sacred moment, and everyone was participating in it.

After Grandfather removed his kerchief from his eyes, Running Bear and his helpers unwound the tobacco bundles from around the four direction flags and handed them to Returning Boy.

"You will want to offer these to Wakan Tanka," Grandfather said. "When the time is right, you might want to do a ceremony and burn them.

"We have given you the name of Returning Boy Who Goes Forward. We know that you not only have returned to us, you will take this wisdom and move forward. The world needs this wisdom. Our ancestors have told us to preserve this wisdom for a time when the world needs it. That time is now, and we trust you to share this wisdom when you are ready. Our support and our prayers are always with you."

Those last words of Grandfather entered Returning Boy like gentle drops of light energy that filled his body and mind. He felt the power of the words and of his new name: Returning Boy Who Goes Forward.

"Now let us feast and celebrate the gifts of the Creator." Grandfather lifted his arms and thanked the Creator for all their blessings, especially the wisdom of the ancestors, the food they were eating, all creation, and Returning Boy Who Goes Forward. He ended the prayer with "Mitakuye oyasin—for all our relatives everywhere, including all our relatives in the spirit world."

Running Bear and his friends moved in beside Returning Boy Who Goes Forward and led him to a place of honor beside Grandfather. His food was brought to him. *At last!* he thought. *A chance to taste wild turnip and buffalo stew!* It was delicious! Such a feast—and all provided by the Creator!

Finally, it was time to go.

Grandfather stood up, put his hands on the shoulders of Returning Boy Who Goes Forward, and looked deep into his eyes. "Remember, Returning Boy, anytime you want or need to come back, you can. Spirit Horse will always be with you, and she can always bring you back. You have much life to live and much to learn in your world, and you have much more to learn from your ancestors. Wakan Tanka, the Creator, will always guide your path. We do not say goodbye. We only say, 'Until I see you again': *Toksa ake waein yan kin kte yelo.*"

Returning Boy Who Goes Forward felt much stronger and taller after his ceremony. Although he was not quite eleven years old, he knew he was becoming a man and was helping to carry the wisdom of his people. He hugged his grandfather and then turned and looked at his people. He knew they depended upon him to use his wisdom wisely.

Returning Boy clutched his ceremonial tobacco bundles in his hand, and he and Running Bear strode toward their horses. There seemed to be no reason for words as they walked together. Both swung up onto their horses and headed toward the next day.

Suddenly, Returning Boy Who Goes Forward pulled back on the reins of Spirit Horse and sat looking around his land. This *was* his land. This was the land of his people. He belonged.

"Running Bear, do you think it would be all right if I took a few of these plants and a rock back with me?"

"Of course. Only remember to say a prayer for each thing you take, and leave a gift."

Returning Boy reached into his pockets and pulled out an assortment of found things: matches, a piece of glass, and a seed.

"Those will be just fine," said Running Bear.

Returning Boy gathered what he wanted from the land and jumped back onto Spirit Horse. When they reached their parting place, he and Running Bear slid off their horses. They both knew they would always be together, even if they never saw each other again.

Returning Boy reached out and hugged Running Bear, and they hugged through the centuries.

"*Toksa ake waein yan kin kte yelo.* At another time and place, we will be together again."

The boys repeated their farewell to each other.

Returning Boy Who Goes Forward hugged Spirit Horse and rubbed her nose. "Toksa ake waein yan kin kte yelo," he said as she nickered and nuzzled into him.

# Chapter 7

Tommy woke up early on Christmas Day, feeling eager. He wanted to finish his project and wrap it. *I'm so excited!* he thought. *This is going to be the best Christmas ever!* He had forgotten about what gift he wanted to get. He was too excited about his present for his parents.

Tommy finished his project and wrapped it in his brightly decorated newspaper. It looked beautiful. He was so proud of it. He wrapped one other small package and waited.

Finally, he heard his parents stir, and he was so eager to give them their presents that he could hardly stand to wait any longer. He was all dressed, with his hair combed and teeth brushed, by the time they got up.

Dad and Mom came out of their bedroom. There was still some sadness in their eyes, but they tried to smile when they saw Tommy's excitement.

*They think I am expecting to get that old red bicycle,* thought Tommy. *They think that's why I'm so excited. I don't need that bicycle. I have Spirit Horse. Just wait until they see what I have for them!* Tommy smiled to himself as he thought of his project. He had left it in his room. He wanted to bring it in after he opened his presents. He wanted them to be surprised.

"Come on, Tommy. Let's see what's here for you," Dad said, trying to sound jovial. He was still in his wheelchair, although he had begun to try to walk occasionally to strengthen his legs.

Tommy saw four packages wrapped on the living room chair. Two were obviously from the firefighters' fund. He knew about that, but he didn't care.

He sat down on the floor with his parents, and Mother and Dad sat close. He unwrapped each package slowly, savoring the process, helping his parents to savor it too, and being careful not to tear the paper, as he knew they would use it again. Now he knew that one way to honor the Creator was not to waste anything. Before, he had thought it was silly to be so careful with Christmas paper.

"Socks! Oh, aren't they great? Look at those colors!" said Tommy. "Thanks, Mom. Thanks, Dad." He took each pair lovingly in his hands and looked at them carefully. He then gently passed each pair to his parents for them to admire.

Tommy's parents were touched by his obvious appreciation of each gift.

Next, he opened the package containing his new jeans. "Wow! Jeans! I really need some new jeans." He stood up and held them up. "Great. They're just a little big. That gives me room to grow. I have a feeling I'm going to be growing a lot soon. They're great!"

After he had looked them over carefully and checked all the pockets, the legs, and the belt loops, he handed them to his parents. He could see that his parents were beginning to relax and enjoy his enthusiasm.

He then went for the long package. "A baseball bat! I've always wanted my own bat." He carefully checked what kind it was and looked for the signature on the bat. Then he gripped it with both hands and swung it a bit. "It feels great. It's just right. Feel how smooth it is, and look at that grain. It's a good one."

His father's eyes shone as Tommy handed the bat to him to inspect.

"I bet I know what this last one is," Tommy said, grinning. "Just as I thought—a baseball. Fantastic! Wait'll the other kids see that I have my own ball and bat." Tommy was having a wonderful time, and so were his parents.

He carefully took the ball out of the box and got the feel of it in his hand. It felt good. He liked the weight and the hardness of it. He squeezed it and then handed it to his father. He could see old memories cross his father's face as he took the ball. He would have to ask his father about that sometime.

Tommy carefully folded all the wrapping paper. Then he stood up and said, "Now I have some presents for you. I would really like it if you could sit on the couch side by side, because I want you to look at this together."

Tommy's father moved to the couch and put the lock on his wheelchair. Taking hold of the arm of the couch and the wheelchair, he moved himself to the couch.

Tommy's mom moved over close to him. It was good to see them close. They both seemed happier than Tommy had seen them in a long time.

"Now, wait right there. Don't move. I'll be right back."

Tommy ran to his room and grabbed his two packages. He hurried back to the living room and presented the bigger of the two packages to them. "Now, unwrap it together," he said as he handed it to them.

"Oh, it's beautiful!" said his mother.

"Did you do this by yourself?" said his father.

"I sure did," said Tommy, expanding with pride.

His parents slowly unwrapped the package. There, lying on the open newspaper, was the loveliest book they had ever seen. The cover was beautiful, and the printing was so clear. "What a beautiful book! *Spirit Horse!*" his father said.

"Please read it before you say anything," said Tommy. He looked intently at his mother and father.

Both his parents tenderly felt the cover of the book. Tommy's drawing was so magnificent that both had tears in their eyes.

"*Spirit Horse* by Returning Boy Who Goes Forward," read his father. Tommy's father knew his language.

His parents read slowly, caressing every page with their eyes and their fingers. Many times, they had to stop to wipe tears from their eyes. Tommy waited.

On the last page, Tommy had glued the plants and the rock he had brought back from their land, the land of his people. He watched as his father gently reached out and touched each plant, calling them all by their Lakota names. Tears streamed down his face.

His mother too reached out and touched the stone and the plants, and her cheeks were wet with tears. "Tommy, Returning Boy, this is the greatest gift we have ever had!"

"We have been alone," his father said. "We have been so isolated. We have not been proud of who we are.

"We have a land.

"We have a heritage.

"We have a people.

"We will never be alone again.

"This is the most healing gift we could ever have."

They sat quietly for a long time. Then Tommy produced his other package and gave it to his parents.

As his parents opened the package, their faces registered surprise and joy, and then tears graced their eyes again.

"Your tobacco bundles. We must go do a ceremony and offer them to Wakan Tanka," his father said, carefully standing up and heading for the door.

Tommy took his mother's hand as they followed. "Mother, get the matches. We must offer these tobacco bundles to the Creator. Mitakuye oyasin—for all our relations."

# Afterword

The original version of *Not Just a Collection of Short Stories* was in the process of being published when Dr. Anne Wilson Schaef passed away of cancer in January 2020 at the age of eighty-five. She had submitted the book many months earlier and received twenty-seven pages of editorial evaluation back from the publisher when she began her chemotherapy treatments. As you might surmise from this wonderful book of poems and short stories, Anne had a vast array of experiences, knowledge, and wisdom and always had her hands in many pots.

She was busy up until the end of her life, as she was the president of two international corporations, had numerous book ideas and writing projects going, was facilitating an international training group in the work she taught called Living in Process, and oversaw several properties, among other things. While she loved to write—and frequently talked about the book she was going to write on cancer, the disease that killed her—she was never fond of the editing process. When the editorial evaluation came back from the publisher, she grimaced, as she always did, and seemingly put the pages on her desk to be buried away forever.

To my surprise, she must have dug up the twenty-seven pages at some point and looked at the editorial feedback, as she started talking about some of the editorial notes. She was particularly struck by one comment that said, "It is unusual to find both of these kinds of content (children and adult) in a single volume, which may make it difficult to market this book. The author is strongly encouraged to choose a specific audience—adults, children, or young adults—and to revise the manuscript with this audience in mind."

While marketing books was never Anne's primary focus or purpose, she did think the editorial staff had a point. In the final months of her life, as she struggled to do even the most basic things, like take a shower, she never lost the great wisdom she had. Those of us who were close to her often marveled at the gems that would come out of her mouth as she began to fade. One day she walked out of her room and said, "I've got it!"

Not knowing what *it* was, as she came out with new ideas constantly, I braced myself and said, "Yes?"

"I know how to fix the short stories book!"

"Great!" I said. "And what are you going to do?"

"I'm going to make it into two books! I will take out all the children's stories and have a second book focusing on children."

"Fantastic!" I said, and I felt relieved that she would be able to get the books finished so I would stop receiving the dozens and dozens of phone calls and emails from the publisher wondering where the book was.

Sadly, she never was able to do it. Her health failed in the coming months, and she eventually passed away peacefully at her home.

Anne had, however, planted the seed for the additional publication and basically had already grown the whole tree. The children's stories were already written; they just needed to be pulled out and put under a second cover.

This is that children's book, and it was the last book Anne completed. We all were especially fond of the story "Spirit Horse" and, over the years, had considered publishing it on its own. When it came to picking a title for this book, this story jumped out as the most significant (and certainly the longest) children's story, so we gave this book that title.

If you've read this far, I hope you enjoyed Anne's work and learned something from her wise words. Anne was always teaching and learning, and she often spoke about her childhood and how her parents and elders were always teaching her and all the young ones. That was their Cherokee way of life.

I think Anne Wilson Schaef was a world treasure. I am honored to have worked and lived with her for the last twenty-five years of her life. Like many others, I have been inspired, moved, and educated and have grown vastly as a human in being with Anne and reading her writing. She was a visionary, and her voice (and pen!) will be missed.

Pete Sidley
Longtime companion, manager, typist, right-hand man
May 2020
Rogers, Arkansas

# About the Author

Anne Wilson Schaef, PhD, is back in the game. This *New York Times* best-selling author, once described as one of the most important thinkers of our time, has returned from her spiritual retreat and time out to get clear. She has had four new books come out recently, with two or three on the way. She is not finished yet. She has broken her silence and is now ready to share her observations, thoughts, and wisdom about individuals; relationships; cultural trends; and the world we have created, in which we are embedded and by which we are acted upon.

With Schaef's previous books, publishers, booksellers, and bookstores always tried to put her into a category—psychology, New Age, women, politics, organizational, addiction—and none or all ever completely fit. At least the publishing world could pigeonhole her as a nonfiction writer. Well, those days are over! Here is her first ever book of children's stories and poems.

As an eighty-five-year-old Cherokee Irish English elder, Schaef has a lot to say about her observations, thoughts, and awarenesses, and what she has to say is more focused than, bigger than, and more inclusive and far reaching than any form or category. With a keen eye, wisdom, and humor, Schaef stands back and observes and fully participates in our world today. Gratefully, she has not succumbed to it. With a piercing awareness and a loving compassion, she "sees" what we have created and reflects it back to us.

In *Spirit Horse and Other Children's Writings*, through poetry and short stories, Schaef ponders our world with us.

Schaef often says, "Don't try to girdle me into a category, form, or pigeonhole. We are all too big for that. Reductionism is out of style. Reductionism has had its run. It's time to expand and expand. Don't be afraid."

Our self-imposed prisons are not necessary. They only give an illusion of safety. Don't be fooled.

Printed in the United States
by Baker & Taylor Publisher Services